INHABITING ETERNITY ON EARTH

DAVID HOPE

ISBN 0-9772194-9-6

ISBN13 978-0-9772194-9-0

Library of Congress Control Number: 2010921830

Printed in the United States of America

RevMedia Publishing
PO BOX 5172
Kingwood, TX 77325

A ministry division of Revelation Ministries

www.revministries.com
www.revmedianetwork.com
www.revmediapublishing.com

CONTENTS

FORWARD

By Roger Dewitt

Pastor Hope does an excellent job with some information that most teachers will not even attempt to relay to his students. "INHABITING ETERNITY ON EARTH" is such an all absorbing teaching that once you read the first few pages you will be fascinated by the potential that is mostly untapped by Christians.

The reader will receive insight about the potential that is given to the blood washed believer. No barrier is too great or no distance too far for the person who can grasp the truths in this easy to read thesis. Don't you think it is about time to take back what the devil stole when he deceived Adam & Eve? After reading and completing this book the reader will have a better understanding of how to move in the supernatural.

The subject has been too long overlooked and Pastor David uses terms and expressions that make it easy to get excited about stepping over into mostly unchartered territory. READ AND BE BLESSED!

PREFACE

The kingdom laws of the spirit realm rule over the natural laws of time, space, and gravity. That's why we hear it said that God is omnipresent. In other words, he is everywhere. He can be everywhere at once because he is not limited by time and space.

God has dominion over time and space because he created them. If you are born again, you too can, by faith, have dominion over time and space through the Holy Ghost. The revelation of that truth in this book may cause you to think that this subject is just a little too way-out for you. You may think that you don't want to participate in having dominion over time and space. But if you are already born again, it is too late to ignore this truth. If you are in Christ, then you are here on the earth and at the same time seated in heavenly places with Christ Jesus. You are already participating in having dominion over time and space as you are in two places at once this very moment!

Stay with me in the journey through this book, and you will find that all miracles involve dominion over natural laws. The more you receive of that revelation the more you will walk in miracles. As you read this book, you will also discover what will prompt Jesus to say that you have great faith. God bless you as you learn these kingdom principles.

INTRODUCTION

Have you ever wondered how God could entertain billions of prayer requests at one time and still give full individual attention to each person? The truth of the answer is difficult for our finite natural mind to grasp, but the concept and the performance of such a task is easy for God because he inhabits eternity. God inhabits eternity past, eternity present and eternity future.

"For thus saith the high and lofty One that inhabiteth eternity, whose name is Holy; I dwell in the high and holy place, with him also that is of a contrite and humble spirit, to revive the spirit of the humble, and to revive the heart of the contrite ones" (Isa. 57:15).

"I am Alpha and Omega, the beginning and the ending, saith the Lord, which is, and which was, and which is to come, the Almighty" (Rev. 1:8).

In the natural world, we live in a chronological time realm, but God does not exist in chronological time. A day and a thousand years are no different to God because he inhabits eternity or, in other words, he lives in the eternal realm.

"But, beloved, be not ignorant of this one thing, that one day is with the Lord as a thousand years, and a thousand years as one day" (2 Pet. 3:8).

In fact, chronological time is just for this earth. When there is a new heaven and a new earth there will be no more time. Everyone will inhabit eternity. God will end the realm of all time as revealed to us in Revelation 10:6.

When God created the earth, he formed Adam and Eve and gave them life. He not only gave them life, he gave them eternal life. They inhabited eternity just like God. They were designed to live forever in bodies that would never wear out. That is why God said that if they ate of the fruit from the tree of the knowledge of good and evil, they would die.

When they ate of that fruit, they did not suddenly die physically, but they moved from living in the eternal realm or *ion* (no time) to *chronos* time (chronological or linear time). They didn't die immediately, but the count down to death began as they started living in linear time, which is finite.

Because they no longer inhabited eternity like God, the door was opened to fear, worry, and anxiety. That is what sin does to people. Did you know that worry and fear are based on time constraints? That is why worry does not exist in the eternal realm. Nobody is worried in heaven. Adam and Eve lived in paradise because they had no worries.

What if you never had a time deadline? Imagine that you were given a difficult and daunting assignment. Now imagine that you have all of eternity to complete it. You won't grow old and can't run out of time. Would you worry? No, because eventually you would find many people willing to teach you, train you, assist you, or just do it for you. If nothing happened today or tomorrow or for the next one million years, you would still have no fewer days to complete your task.

God exists above time and is not controlled by time. Further, he has given his children dominion over time, space, gravity, and all natural laws as we are anointed by the Holy Ghost. God is not limited by time. He told Abraham that he had made (past tense) him a father of many nations before Sarah was pregnant.

"Neither shall thy name any more be called Abram, but thy name shall be Abraham; for a father of many nations have I made thee" (Gen. 17:5).

God is not bound by time. He is the beginning and the end. God gave Abraham the promised son Isaac when Abraham was 100 years old. God then moved back in time to tell Abram about what he had already done. God inhabits the future and knows exactly what is going to happen in your future, even if you set your will against it. Why? He was already there.

Let's look at the situation when Jesus told Peter of his future and how he would deny Jesus that very night, three times, before the rooster crowed.

"Peter answered and said unto him, Though all [men] shall be offended because of thee, yet will I never be offended. Jesus said unto him, Verily I say unto thee, that this night, before the cock crow, thou shalt deny me thrice. Peter said unto him, Though I should die with thee, yet will I not deny thee. Likewise also said all the disciples. Now Peter sat without in the palace: and a damsel came unto him, saying, Thou also wast with Jesus of Galilee. But he denied before them all, saying, I know not what thou sayest. And when he was gone out into the porch, another maid saw him, and said unto them that were there, This fellow was also with Jesus of Nazareth. And again he denied with an oath, I do not know the man. And after a while came unto him they that stood by, and said to Peter, Surely thou also art one of them; for thy speech betrayeth thee. Then began he to curse and to swear, saying, I know not the man. And immediately the cock crew. And Peter remembered the word of Jesus, which said unto him, Before the cock crow, thou shalt deny me thrice. And he went out, and wept bitterly" (Matt. 26:33–35, 69–75).

Jesus stated the exact number of times that Peter would deny him. He also revealed the exact moment in time when Peter would deny him the third time, even though Peter said he would die before he would deny knowing Jesus. Jesus knew it all because he inhabits eternity and is not bound by time.

When you pray, you have God's undivided attention. You can be assured of that because he is always in the present for us. He will minister to you and then go back in time to be in the present for all the others praying at the same time. God is a God of the now. The Bible says in Hebrews 11:7 that "now faith is."

When Adam fell through sin, he fell from revelation to information. He fell from discerning to learning. He fell from eternal to temporal and he fell from dominion over time to being under the pressure of time. Jesus, through his sacrifice on the cross, gave us dominion over the things of this world and over Satan and his kingdom of darkness.

You cannot take dominion over Satan without revelation because Satan has all the information there is. The wisdom of men comes from what you can reason with your mind. Satan has an entire system based on human reasoning. Satan, our enemy, wants to place a false thought pattern inside of you that advances the notion that things of the earth have dominion over you. If he can get that into your spirit, then you will follow those thoughts. For example, if he can produce a shortage in your mind, then you will have a shortage.

"For as he thinketh in his heart, so is he" (Prov. 23:7a).

Satan is bound by time. He has an appointed end. That's why he tries to teach you to think and talk in linear time. That's why you've got to say, "By his [Christ's] stripes I am healed" and not "I will be healed." If you say, "I'm going to be healed," you have taken God's Word and put it into the future. God says it's already done. Therefore, you are not in agreement with God's Word. Jesus operated above time. That is the key to miracles. Our part is to say what God has said as if it is already done, because that is the truth. The fact may be that you are sick, but the truth is "by whose stripes ye were healed" (1 Pet. 2:24b). In other words, if you have a disease, the flu, or a fever, the condition is a natural reality. We should believe that the supernatural kingdom laws override all natural things. When we confess our healing, we believe the higher spiritual truth that we already have our healing. This doesn't automatically happen when we become a member of the family of God. We must choose to believe it and then speak it, knowing that we already have it.

"Therefore I say unto you, What things soever ye desire, when ye pray, believe that ye receive them, and ye shall have them" (Mark 11:24).

When we pray, we believe that we already have what we speak. That is the God kind of faith. By faith we have access to the timeless, eternal realm of God and therefore all the things of God. You can bring them into your life and your life will not be under the pressure of the world. There are all kinds of wonderful blessings and treasures stored in heaven for you and me. God has already blessed you with blessings that include even your future needs and desires. We won't need them in heaven. They are for us

11

while we are still on the earth. They are reserved for you. They have your name on them.

"Blessed be the God and Father of our Lord Jesus Christ, who hath blessed us with all spiritual blessings in heavenly places in Christ" (Eph. 1:3).

"According as his divine power hath given unto us all things that pertain to life and godliness" (2 Pet. 1:3a).

Notice that both of the above Scriptures are in the past tense. That's because God has already blessed us and given them to us. Once you come in to heaven by faith, all time and space is gone. The Bible says we are seated together with Jesus in heavenly places. How can you be seated in heaven and be on the earth at the same time? In heaven, there is no time or space. By faith we take dominion over time and space as God does.

How can you walk in this dominion? You have to renew your mind with the revelation that you, like God, inhabit eternity. The enemy has trained you for linear time. He has trained you to say "One day, I'll reach my goals. Someday, I'll do this and someday I'll do that." This is the way I used to talk. I said, "Someday I'm going to have an inner city street ministry. Someday I'm going to win thousands of souls in Africa, and someday I'm going to sing for the Lord." I said, "Someday I'm going to record a music CD and someday I'm going to write books for the Lord and someday I'm going to be a pastor."

When I stopped talking like that, things changed. When I quit saying "someday" and started saying that I have those things, I started a street ministry. I have been on eight mission trips to Africa and led over 11,000 people to the Lord on those trips, mostly children. I started singing for the Lord in church and recorded a CD. I am now a full-time pastor, and this is my fourth book about the Kingdom of God.

As I saw this principle unfold in my life, I stopped saying, "One day I'll go to heaven" and started saying, "through revelation knowledge today, right now, I have access to heaven to bring the good things of God to the earth." By faith, I can leave time, enter eternity, and access my treasure in heaven that is set aside for me to take to the earth.

"Thy kingdom come. Thy will be done in earth, as it is in heaven" (Matt. 6:10).

As you "call the things that are not as though they were," you will see great miracles in your life!

CHAPTER 1

DOMINION OVER TIME AND SPIRITUAL GIFTS

Many Christians today would not even think about walking on water like Peter, or being translated to another physical location like Philip, or stopping the sun like Joshua. Many do, however, desire to operate in spiritual gifts as described in 1 Corinthians 12:8–10. You may not yet be able to make the decision to take dominion over time, but can you desire to receive a word of wisdom from the Spirit of God?

The spiritual gift of word of wisdom shows you things to come as you receive revelation of future events in linear time from the Spirit of God, who inhabits eternity. As you release your faith for it, you too inhabit eternity. If this is not something real for us today, then why does the devil offer a counterfeit for it with fortunetellers and astrology? If we are not to take dominion over natural laws, then why did Jesus invite Peter to walk on water by saying, "come"? Since Jesus is the same yesterday, today and forever and no respecter of persons, he is inviting you to rise up and take dominion over natural laws, including time, and right now receive what God said is already yours. We should want this blessing from God along with all the other precious gifts of the Spirit.

"But covet earnestly the best gifts" (1 Cor. 12:31a).

God wants to give us a glimpse of the future. Part of the work of the Holy Spirit is to show us things to come. The more we know where we are headed, the less likely we are to become offended and get off track. We become offended when people say and do things that we think will stop us from getting what we want. We can avoid all that by understanding the good place that God says we are going and that no man or devil can stop us. The only thing that can stop us is our own mouth.

"A man's belly shall be satisfied with the fruit of his mouth; and with the increase of his lips shall he be filled. Death and life are in the power of the tongue: and they that love it shall eat the fruit thereof" (Prov. 18:20–21).

We know what God has shown us is not some wild speculation. We know that it has already happened for God inhabits eternity and has merely reported what has taken place ahead in linear time. As a result of this revelation, we don't have to worry if certain things do or do not happen or if certain things are or are not said.

We look at what we are going to instead of what we are going through. We walk in joy because we know we are going to make it no matter what our current circumstances are. We can walk in integrity and in godly character because we don't have to make it happen. There is no need to manipulate people and circumstances to produce what we desire. We simply obey God and believe for the manifestation of the promises of God. "But he who was of the bondwoman was born after the flesh; but he of the freewoman was by promise" (Gal. 4:23).

We can walk through the tough times and not lose our focus on where we are going. I remember when my wife and I made plans to go to Hawaii for our twenty-fifth wedding anniversary. In order to keep the costs down, we planned the trip well in advance. For several months, we talked about and anticipated how great it was going to be. We went through our normal lives dealing with tough

16

problems and issues, yet we had great joy as we looked forward to those beautiful beaches and landscapes. The anticipation of the vacation was almost as good as the vacation itself, yet it lasted much longer!

Another reason why God would want us to know the future is to advance his kingdom by financially blessing his people. I believe God will use the word of wisdom in a big way for the wealth transfer from the wicked to the righteous.

Let's look at an example where God gave a word of wisdom for the financial benefit of his servant in order to advance his kingdom and his people.

"And it came to pass at the end of two full years, that Pharaoh dreamed: and, behold, he stood by the river. And, behold, there came up out of the river seven well favoured kine and fatfleshed; and they fed in a meadow. And, behold, seven other kine came up after them out of the river, ill favoured and leanfleshed; and stood by the other kine upon the brink of the river. And the ill favoured and leanfleshed kine did eat up the seven well favoured and fat kine. So Pharaoh awoke. And he slept and dreamed the second time: and, behold, seven ears of corn came up upon one stalk, rank and good. And, behold, seven thin ears and blasted with the east wind sprung up after them. And the seven thin ears devoured the seven rank and full ears. And Pharaoh awoke, and, behold, it was a dream. And it came to pass in the morning that his spirit was troubled; and he sent and called for all the magicians of Egypt, and all the wise men thereof: and Pharaoh told them his dream; but there was none that could interpret them unto Pharaoh. Then spake the chief butler unto Pharaoh, saying, I do remember my faults this day: Pharaoh was wroth with his servants, and put me in ward in the captain of the guard's house, both me and the chief baker: And we dreamed a dream in one night, I and he; we dreamed each man according to the interpretation of his dream. And there was there with us a young man, an Hebrew, servant to the captain of the guard; and we told him, and he interpreted to us our dreams; to each man according to his dream he did interpret. And it came to pass, as he interpreted to us, so it was; me he restored unto mine office, and him he hanged. Then Pharaoh sent and called Joseph, and they brought him hastily out of the dungeon: and he shaved himself, and changed his raiment, and came in unto Pharaoh. And Pharaoh said unto Joseph, I have dreamed a dream, and there is none that can interpret it: and I have heard say of thee, that thou canst understand a dream to interpret it" (Gen. 41:1–15).

Joseph was in that prison because of several wrongful acts done to him by various people, including his own brothers. Joseph's brothers were jealous of Joseph because he was the favorite of their father. They were also envious that Joseph dared to dream big dreams. Joseph was sold into slavery to the Medianites by his brothers for twenty pieces of silver. The Medianites brought Joseph into Egypt and sold him to Potiphar, an officer of Pharaoh and captain of the guard. Potiphar's wife falsely accused Joseph and Potiphar had Joseph put into prison—the inner prison where the prisoners are kept bound.

God had told Joseph through his dream that Joseph was going to do great things. I'm sure that as Joseph sat in that inner prison, it didn't look too promising for those dreams to come true. Joseph didn't stop believing and didn't stop being faithful, because he knew his destiny. He had a word from God. He had a vision from God. He kept looking at what he was going to and not at what he was going through.

You may have quit being faithful because someone has done you wrong. Arise and be faithful to God, for no one has done you wrong like what was done to Joseph by his own brothers. God still has great plans and dreams for you. Remember this, while you are being faithful, God is working behind the scenes to bring blessing and favor into your life.

Moments before Pharaoh summoned him, Joseph was at his very lowest. Yet, he was only a few hours away from being placed in charge of all of Egypt. Joseph went from the proverbial outhouse to the penthouse in the very same day. Don't give up on the dream God has given you. Joseph did what it takes for a dream from God to come true. He kept believing and didn't give up. He was faithful wherever he was, even at his lowest point and even though people had treated him unfairly.

Then Pharaoh asked Joseph to interpret his dream and God, who inhabits eternity, gives Joseph a look at the future for the next fourteen years. Joseph knows exactly what was going to happen to the food supply and gives Pharaoh an exact interpretation of his dream.

"Behold, there come seven years of great plenty throughout all the land of Egypt: And there shall arise after them seven years of famine; and all the plenty shall be forgotten in the land of Egypt; and the famine shall consume the land; And the plenty shall not be known in the land by reason of that famine following; for it shall be very grievous. And for that the dream was doubled unto Pharaoh twice; it is because the thing is established by God, and God will shortly bring it to pass. Now therefore let Pharaoh look out a man discreet and wise, and set him over the land of Egypt. Let Pharaoh do this, and let him appoint officers over the land, and take up the fifth part of the land of Egypt in the seven plenteous years. And let them gather all the food of those good years that come, and lay up corn under the hand of Pharaoh, and let them keep food in the cities. And that food shall be for store to the land against the seven years of famine, which shall be in the land of Egypt; that the land perish not through the famine. And the thing was good in the eyes of Pharaoh, and in the eyes of all his servants. And Pharaoh said unto his servants, Can we find such a one as this is, a man in whom the Spirit of God is? And Pharaoh said unto Joseph, Forasmuch as God hath shewed thee all this, there is none so discreet and wise as thou art: Thou shalt be over my house, and according unto thy word shall all my people be ruled: only in the throne will I be greater than thou. And Pharaoh said unto Joseph, See, I have set thee over all the land of Egypt. And Pharaoh took off his ring from his hand, and put it upon Joseph's hand, and arrayed him in vestures of fine linen, and put a gold chain about his neck; And he made him to ride in the second chariot which he had; and they cried before him, Bow the knee: and he made him ruler over all the land of Egypt. And Pharaoh said unto Joseph, I am Pharaoh, and without thee shall no man lift up his hand or foot in all the land of Egypt" (Gen. 41:29–44).

Think about this. In the morning, Joseph was stinky, hairy, starving, and sitting in chains in the inner prison with no prospects of ever seeing the light of day again. By the afternoon, Joseph was cleaned up, shaved, dressed in robes, and put in charge of everything. That was only the beginning of what God had done in his life in making Joseph's dream come true.

"And the seven years of plenteousness, that was in the land of Egypt, were ended. And the seven years of dearth began to come, according as Joseph had said: and the dearth was in all lands; but in all the land of Egypt there was bread. And when all the land of Egypt was famished, the people cried to Pharaoh for bread: and

Pharaoh said unto all the Egyptians, Go unto Joseph; what he saith to you, do" (Gen. 41:53–55).

Just a few moments of inhabiting eternity brought all this and more. Let's see what happened when the famine kicked in. Remember that Joseph had ordered the excess stored during the time of plenty.

"And he gathered up all the food of the seven years, which were in the land of Egypt, and laid up the food in the cities: the food of the field, which was round about every city, laid he up in the same. And Joseph gathered corn as the sand of the sea, very much, until he left numbering; for it was without number" (Gen. 41:48–49).

Joseph gained complete control, of not only Egypt, but of the whole known world, because of the drought.

"And the famine was over all the face of the earth: and Joseph opened all the storehouses, and sold unto the Egyptians; and the famine waxed sore in the land of Egypt. And all countries came into Egypt to Joseph for to buy corn; because that the famine was so sore in all lands" (Gen. 41:56–57).

Joseph got all the money in the world put under his stewardship.

"And Joseph gathered up all the money that was found in the land of Egypt, and in the land of Canaan, for the corn which they bought: and Joseph brought the money into Pharaoh's house" (Gen. 47:14).

When the people had no more money, their hunger caused them to give up all their livestock for food.

"And when money failed in the land of Egypt, and in the land of Canaan, all the Egyptians came unto Joseph, and said, Give us bread: for why should we die in thy presence? For the money faileth. And Joseph said, Give your cattle; and I will give you for your cattle, if money fail. And they brought their cattle unto Joseph: and Joseph gave them bread in exchange for horses, and for the flocks, and for the cattle of the herds, and for the asses: and he fed them with bread for all their cattle for that year" (Gen. 47:15–17).

When the people had no more money or cattle, their hunger caused them to give up all their land.

"When that year was ended, they came unto him the second year, and said unto him, We will not hide it from my lord, how that our money is spent; my lord also hath our herds of cattle; there is not ought left in the sight of my lord, but our bodies, and our lands: Wherefore shall we die before thine eyes, both we and our land? Buy us and our land for bread, and we and our land will be servants unto Pharaoh: and give us seed, that we may live, and not die, that the land be not desolate. And Joseph bought all the land of Egypt for Pharaoh; for the Egyptians sold every man his field, because the famine prevailed over them: so the land became Pharaoh's" (Gen. 47:18–20).

When Joseph had all the money, all the livestock, and all the land, he sold food for 20 percent of their future income.

"Then Joseph said unto the people, Behold, I have bought you this day and your land for Pharaoh: lo, here is seed for you, and ye shall sow the land. And it shall come to pass in the increase, that ye shall give the fifth part unto Pharaoh, and four parts shall be your own, for seed of the field, and for your food, and for them of your households, and for food for your little ones. And they said, Thou hast saved our lives: let us find grace in the sight of my lord, and we will be Pharaoh's servants" (Gen. 47:23–25).

All of the world's money, cattle, land, and 20 percent of future income of the world came into the hands and discretion of Joseph, all from one word of wisdom from God Almighty who inhabits eternity. What could God do with your life if he gave you a glimpse of the future? Consider your current situation and resources compared to that of Joseph when he received the word of wisdom from God.

Simply by believing that these things are for the body of Christ today, you too can walk in the supernatural kingdom principles as they override natural laws. Don't wait until you feel comfortable to enter in. If you do, you will never enter in. No one is very comfortable when he or she first desires to be baptized in the Holy Ghost. Do you remember the first time you raised your hands in church? How comfortable did you feel? How do you feel about it now? The supernatural should not seem strange to us because that is normal in our real home in heaven where we have our real citizenship.

Don't try to make things happen in your own might and power. We need the supernatural to bring the good things of heaven down to the earth.

"Not by might, nor by power, but by my spirit, saith the LORD of hosts" (Zech. 4:6b).

God knows what is going to go up in value and what is going to go down in value. He knows exactly when things are going up and down in value. God is already using the ability to show his servants the future to bring about the end-time wealth transfer to those who please him and will inhabit eternity with him by faith. What will prompt God to give us such information? Let's learn more about the end-time wealth transfer.

CHAPTER 2

END-TIME WEALTH TRANSFER

A transfer of wealth has always been available to God's people who could receive the revelation of this principle by faith. I believe this transfer will be accelerated in these last days.

"For God giveth to a man that is good in his sight wisdom, and knowledge, and joy: but to the sinner he giveth travail, to gather and to heap up, that he may give to him that is good before God" (Eccl. 2:26a).

"A good man leaveth an inheritance to his children's children: and the wealth of the sinner is laid up for the just" (Prov. 13:22).

"For thus saith the LORD of hosts; Yet once, it is a little while, and I will shake the heavens, and the earth, and the sea, and the dry land; And I will shake all nations, and the desire of all nations shall come: and I will fill this house with glory, saith the LORD of hosts. The silver is mine, and the gold is mine, saith the LORD of hosts. The glory of this latter house shall be greater than of the former, saith the LORD of hosts: and in this place will I give peace, saith the LORD of hosts" (Hag. 2:6–9).

Some people believe that there should be a wealth transfer from those who have to those who have not. This is a counterfeit from Satan, and such a notion is contrary to the Word of God.

"And he said unto them that stood by, Take from him the pound, and give it to him that hath ten pounds. (And they said unto him,

Lord, he hath ten pounds.) For I say unto you, That unto every one which hath shall be given; and from him that hath not, even that he hath shall be taken away from him" (Luke 19:24–26).

I believe that the accelerated end-time wealth transfer has, at the time of this writing, just entered its infant stage. For the full manifestation of this event, God's people must take dominion over time. This is one of the main reasons I wrote this book. The transfer won't be from the rich to the poor; it won't even be from the lost to the saved. It will be from those who are afraid to work kingdom principles to those who are walking the narrow way, working according to kingdom principles, and thereby gaining by trading.

Let's study Luke 19:12–26, which reveals to us Jesus' parable of the ten pieces of money. The principles revealed in this parable have always been in the earth and vital for our prosperity in the Lord, but they are especially important in these last days. I will explain why later in this chapter.

"He said therefore, a certain nobleman went into a far country to receive for himself a kingdom, and to return. And he called his ten servants, and delivered them ten pounds, and said unto them, Occupy till I come. But his citizens hated him, and sent a message after him, saying, We will not have this man to reign over us" (Luke19:12–14).

The certain nobleman is, of course, Jesus. He left this earth to receive his kingdom and he will someday return. His citizens indeed hated and rejected him.

"He came unto his own, and his own received him not" (John 1:11).

"He is despised and rejected of men; a man of sorrows, and acquainted with grief: and we hid as it were our faces from him; he was despised, and we esteemed him not" (Isa. 53:3).

Notice that he called his servants, not the ungodly. This parable is about God's people. Each servant got one pound, and each of them were to occupy or put the pound to work until his return.

"And it came to pass, that when he was returned, having received the kingdom, then he commanded these servants to be called unto him, to whom he had given the money, that he might know how much every man had gained by trading" (Luke 19:15).

Please notice that Jesus was talking about money. This parable is all about how we handle our money. One day, when Jesus returns, he is going to ask us about how we handled the money he gave us. Notice he didn't ask how much money his servants had. He didn't ask how much they gained through the work of their hands. He wanted to know how much gain or increase they produced, and it wasn't just any increase, but how much they gained by trading. In other words, how much increase did they generate by investing the money that he had entrusted into their hands.

"Then came the first, saying, Lord, thy pound hath gained ten pounds. And he said unto him, Well, thou good servant: because thou hast been faithful in a very little, have thou authority over ten cities" (Luke 19:16–17).

Please notice the increase of ten pounds. When his master saw the increase, he was so pleased that he rewarded him directly proportional to his gain or increase.

"And the second came, saying, Lord, thy pound hath gained five pounds. And he said likewise to him, Be thou also over five cities" (Luke 19:18–19).

This servant was also rewarded according to the increase that he had developed through investing.

"And another came, saying, Lord, behold, here is thy pound, which I have kept laid up in a napkin: For I feared thee, because thou art an austere man: thou takest up that thou layedst not down, and reapest that thou didst not sow. And he saith unto him, Out of thine own mouth will I judge thee, thou wicked servant. Thou knewest that I was an austere man, taking up that I laid not down, and reaping that I did not sow" (Luke 19:20–22).

This servant did not invest because of fear. Fear is always the reason we don't invest. When we turn down an investment opportunity, it is because we are afraid that we will lose what we do have while we are trying to make a gain. Fear is the factor that stops investments. Fear was the result of a lack of knowledge and trust of the nobleman.

"Wherefore then gavest not thou my money into the bank, that at my coming I might have required mine own with usury?" (Luke 19:23).

Banks pay interest or increase. Jesus is interested in increase. He must be interested in us having an increase or he wouldn't have given them a city for every pound they gained.

"And he said unto them that stood by, Take from him the pound, and give it to him that hath ten pounds. (And they said unto him, Lord, he hath ten pounds)" (Luke 19:24–25).

Why didn't he give it to the one that gained five pounds? Here is the point that Jesus is making. The one that works his system the best is the one that gets what the man that walks in fear loses. They were shocked that he gave it to the one that had the most increase. The disciples needed their minds renewed in this area and so do many Christians. Remember, this parable was about God's servants spoken to God's servants. The disciples needed to understand the kingdom way of talking and doing things. They had a "Robin Hood mentality" that they had to get rid of, because that is just a counterfeit way of thinking that originated from Satan. Jesus revealed his kingdom way of thinking to his servants.

"For I say unto you, That unto every one which hath shall be given; and from him that hath not, even that he hath shall be taken away from him" (Luke 19:26).

This is one of the principles of the kingdom that God's people are to know and understand. It is a mystery to the ungodly.

"And the disciples came, and said unto him, Why speakest thou unto them in parables? He answered and said unto them, Because it is given unto you to know the mysteries of the kingdom of heaven, but to them it is not given. For whosoever hath, to him shall be given, and he shall have more abundance: but whosoever hath not, from him shall be taken away even that he hath. Therefore speak I to them in parables: because they seeing see not; and hearing they hear not, neither do they understand" (Matt. 13:10–13).

Don't think like the lost and miss out on the end-time wealth transfer. Jesus wants you to invest in the kingdom of God, and he guarantees you great increase and no chance of a loss, for the kingdom is good ground. No earthly endeavor can make such a promise.

"But other fell into good ground, and brought forth fruit, some an hundredfold, some sixtyfold, some thirtyfold. Who hath ears to hear, let him hear" (Matt. 13:8).

"But lay up for yourselves treasures in heaven, where neither moth nor rust doth corrupt, and where thieves do not break through nor steal" (Matt 6:20).

Even servants of God who walk in fear are going to lose what Jesus is offering them, and it will go to the one who will walk in faith and believe for the increase. This is a principle that God has put into the earth. I'm not saying it's wrong to make an earthly investment. You will need those as you receive the supernatural increase or gain by trading from working this principle.

Let me explain it in detail. Let's read verse 26 again.

"For I say unto you, That unto every one which hath shall be given; and from him that hath not, even that he hath shall be taken away from him" (Luke 19:26).

How can someone who "hath not" have something taken away. What we have or have not is increase. That is what Jesus was talking about. What he wanted to know was this: how much every man gained by trading. In other words, Jesus will ask us how much increase did we allow him to give us by investing in the kingdom of God. In the way we talk today, the principle can be stated like this:

Everyone that has received increase through giving (investing) money into the Kingdom of God will be given more money. This additional money will come from the ones who received no increase from God because they were afraid to put their money into the Kingdom. The money they held back because of fear will go into the hands of those who know how to generate increase from God so they can continue to support and advance God's Kingdom.

In the lasts days, the manifestation of this "mystery" will take less time to produce fruit. That means that the time between sowing a seed and reaping a harvest will take less time. As we obey God, we will be able to accomplish in a short time what used to take a much longer time. Partner with God, take dominion over time, and accomplish in one year what seems to the natural mind to take ten years. It's not too late for your dreams to come true.

"Behold, the days come, saith the LORD, that the plowman shall overtake the reaper, and the treader of grapes him that soweth seed; and the mountains shall drop sweet wine, and all the hills shall melt" (Amos 9:13).

I believe the days have come when the harvester comes right on the heels of the sower as we take dominion over time by faith. The plowman is making ready for new seeds on the heels of the reaper. Don't stop your faithfulness. Don't think you are too old for your dreams to come true. Realize that God has dominion over time and by faith so do you. Continue to dream big dreams. Now is not the time to quit; instead, go forward with renewed faith, for God has made a way for you to fulfill your kingdom destiny.

The devil can't stop you. Your revelation of dominion over time beats his information of your age every time. Keep looking at what you are going to, continue to be faithful right where you are, sow more seeds than ever before, don't quit and the victory is automatically yours!

"And let us not be weary in well doing: for in due season we shall reap, if we faint not" (Gal. 6:9).

CHAPTER 3

DOMINION OVER TIME AND SPACE IN THE MINISTRY OF JESUS

Every miracle in Jesus' earthly ministry involved dominion over natural laws, especially those of linear time. It happened in the first miracle mentioned (water into wine) and the last one mentioned (in the twinkling of an eye) and virtually each one in between. That shows us that many of our miracles today involve dominion over time. Don't you think we should get a revelation of this truth if we want to walk in the full power of our inheritance?

Jesus came down to our level to rescue us. He didn't come to stay low with us but to bring us back up to his level. Through his blood he made a way of escape and victory for you and me so that we may live at his level as a joint equal heir of his kingdom.

"For ye know the grace of our Lord Jesus Christ, that, though he was rich, yet for your sakes he became poor, that ye through his poverty might be rich" (2 Cor. 8:9).

"The Spirit itself beareth witness with our spirit, that we are the children of God: And if children, then heirs; heirs of God, and joint-heirs with Christ" (Rom. 8:16–17a).

"But God, who is rich in mercy, for his great love wherewith he loved us, Even when we were dead in sins, hath quickened us together with Christ, (by grace ye are saved;) And hath raised us up together, and made us sit together in heavenly places in Christ Jesus That in the ages to come he might shew the exceeding riches of his grace in his kindness toward us through Christ Jesus. For by grace are ye saved through faith; and that not of yourselves: it is the gift of God: Not of works, lest any man should boast" (Eph. 2:4–9).

Jesus inhabits eternity, so when we are born again by the Spirit we are born into the eternal realm so that we never really die and we too inhabit eternity just as God does. Jesus tried to explain this to the Jews, but they would not hear because of the hardness of their hearts.

"Your father Abraham rejoiced to see my day: and he saw it, and was glad. Then said the Jews unto him, Thou art not yet fifty years old, and hast thou seen Abraham? Jesus said unto them, Verily, verily, I say unto you, Before Abraham was, I am. Then took they up stones to cast at him: but Jesus hid himself, and went out of the temple, going through the midst of them, and so passed by" (John. 8:56–59).

Jesus didn't walk bound by time, and we as his people don't have to either. I'm not talking about always being late for appointments. Integrity and faith go together and we should always keep our word. I'm talking about how Abraham saw ahead in time. What was it that Abraham saw? He saw Jesus' day. In other words, he saw ahead in time when God was manifested in the flesh. God can reveal any portion of linear time to his children because we inhabit eternity through Jesus Christ. Because Jesus lives, we live also. Jesus inhabits eternity. That's how he could take on all the sins of humanity from every age on the earth at one moment in time. Since we are in Christ, we too inhabit eternity and can live in that realm.

Jesus said that before Abraham was, I Am. God told Moses to say that I Am sent him. God is always in the now for you and me. That's why he is the same yesterday, today, and forever. There is no time in the eternal realm.

I told you in the preface that I would show you what could prompt Jesus to say that you have great faith. The Bible records only two instances where Jesus made this statement about someone. Let's read about them. The first is the centurion.

"And when Jesus was entered into Capernaum, there came unto him a centurion, beseeching him, And saying, Lord, my servant lieth at home sick of the palsy, grievously tormented. And Jesus saith unto him, I will come and heal him. The centurion answered and said, Lord, I am not worthy that thou shouldest come under my roof: but speak the word only, and my servant shall be healed. For I am a man under authority, having soldiers under me: and I say to this man, Go, and he goeth; and to another, Come, and he cometh; and to my servant, Do this, and he doeth it. When Jesus heard it, he marvelled, and said to them that followed, Verily I say unto you, I have not found so great faith, no, not in Israel. And Jesus said unto the centurion, Go thy way; and as thou hast believed, so be it done unto thee. And his servant was healed in the selfsame hour" (Matt. 8:5–10, 13).

Jesus said the centurion had great faith. The other was a woman of Canaan.

"And, behold, a woman of Canaan came out of the same coasts, and cried unto him, saying, Have mercy on me, O Lord, thou Son of David; my daughter is grievously vexed with a devil. But he answered her not a word. And his disciples came and besought him, saying, Send her away; for she crieth after us. But he answered and said, I am not sent but unto the lost sheep of the house of Israel. Then came she and worshipped him, saying, Lord, help me. But he answered and said, It is not meet to take the children's bread, and to cast it to dogs. And she said, Truth, Lord: yet the dogs eat of the crumbs which fall from their masters' table. Then Jesus answered and said unto her, O woman, great is thy faith: be it unto thee even as thou wilt. And her daughter was made whole from that very hour" (Matt. 15:22–28).

These are the only times that Jesus said someone had great faith. He routinely told his disciples that they had little faith. Jesus also said that we can do a lot with a little faith. Just think what we can do with great faith.

"And Jesus said unto them, Because of your unbelief: for verily I say unto you, If ye have faith as a grain of mustard seed, ye shall say unto this mountain, Remove hence to yonder place; and it shall remove; and nothing shall be impossible unto you" (Matt. 17:20).

Nothing shall be impossible to you, not even moving a mountain from one place to another because by faith we have dominion over time and space.

The woman of Canaan and the centurion took dominion over time and space, and as a result, Jesus said that they had great faith. Since Jesus is the same yesterday, today and forever and no respecter of persons, he will say you have great faith when you take dominion over time and space. That should motivate you to receive the revelation that I am sharing with you. Let me explain it further, starting with the woman of Canaan.

When the woman asked Jesus to heal her daughter, he replied that she was asking for the children's bread. In other words, she was asking for that which belonged to the people in covenant with him. It was not yet time for the new covenant that would include Gentiles such as this woman and her daughter. At that time, Jesus was only sent unto the lost sheep of the house of Israel. Jesus told her that it was not proper to give the children's bread to dogs or to people outside of the covenant. She agreed but said, "Yet the dogs eat the crumbs which fall from the master's table."

This woman took dominion over time and by faith moved ahead in time when the Gentiles could receive healing under the new and better covenant. She had the revelation that healing was the "children's bread." She took dominion over time and space, for she and her daughter were Gentiles, but her daughter was not physically present. The emphasis is on moving ahead in time, and yet she still had to take dominion over space for her daughter to be healed.

The centurion took dominion over time and space, but the emphasis was on dominion over space. When Jesus said that he would come and heal his servant, the centurion said, "Speak the word only, and my servant shall be healed." The Roman captain took dominion over space, as he knew that his servant did not need to be present physically to be healed. Yet the centurion and his servant were both Gentiles, and so the centurion also had to go ahead in time, by faith, for his servant to receive Christ's healing. Both the woman of Canaan and the centurion took dominion over time and space. Both heard Jesus say they had great faith, and both the daughter and the servant were healed that very hour.

Jesus said that we could do the things that he did and even greater. He really meant it when he said we could do the impossible. Let's look at an example of Jesus doing the impossible.

"Then said Martha unto Jesus, Lord, if thou hadst been here, my brother had not died. But I know, that even now, whatsoever thou wilt ask of God, God will give it thee. Jesus saith unto her, Thy brother shall rise again. Martha saith unto him, I know that he shall rise again in the resurrection at the last day. Jesus said unto her, I am the resurrection, and the life: he that believeth in me, though he were dead, yet shall he live" (John 11:21–25).

Jesus is the Alpha and the Omega, the beginning and the end. He has dominion over time, and he wants us to know that his resurrection power is not just at the last day, but also for us right now. Have you ever heard the expression that you can't unscramble eggs? God says that all things are possible with him and that means that he can unscramble eggs. He can take the eggs back in time before they were scrambled and then bring them to the present for us to use as we wish. That's exactly what he did with the body of Lazarus.

"Jesus said, Take ye away the stone. Martha, the sister of him that was dead, saith unto him, Lord, by this time he stinketh: for he hath been dead four days. Jesus saith unto her, Said I not unto thee, that, if thou wouldest believe, thou shouldest see the glory of God? Then they took away the stone from the place where the dead was laid. And Jesus lifted up his eyes, and said, Father, I thank thee that thou hast heard me. And I knew that thou hearest me always: but because of the people which stand by I said it, that they may believe that thou hast sent me. And when he thus had spoken, he cried with a loud voice, Lazarus, come forth. And he that was dead came forth, bound hand and foot with graveclothes: and his face was bound about with a napkin. Jesus saith unto them, Loose him, and let him go. Then many of the Jews which came to Mary, and had seen the things which Jesus did, believed on him" (John. 11:39–45).

When Lazarus came forth, he did not stink. Why? Jesus took his body back to when it was healthy and brought it forward to that time to be with his sisters and Jesus to show everyone that Jesus is Lord. Lazarus wasn't just alive. His body had no signs of decomposition. The grave clothes came off and he was loosed!

Resurrection power was no problem to Jesus then, and it still is no problem to him today. It is available in our finances, our ministries, and even our marriages. Jesus can take a dead marriage, and through dominion over time, take it back to when it was healthy with right hearts. He can bring it forward to today, and it won't stink!

Let's look at another example of Jesus raising someone from the dead.

"While he spake these things unto them, behold, there came a certain ruler, and worshipped him, saying, My daughter is even now dead: but come and lay thy hand upon her, and she shall live. And Jesus arose, and followed him, and so did his disciples. And, behold, a woman, which was diseased with an issue of blood twelve years, came behind him, and touched the hem of his garment: For she said within herself, If I may but touch his garment, I shall be whole. But Jesus turned him about, and when he saw her, he said, Daughter, be of good comfort; thy faith hath made thee whole. And the woman was made whole from that hour. And when Jesus came into the ruler's house, and saw the minstrels and the people making a noise, He said unto them, Give place: for the maid is not dead, but sleepeth. And they laughed him to scorn. But when the people were put forth, he went in, and took her by the hand, and the maid arose. And the fame hereof went abroad into all that land" (Matt. 9:18–26).

It was not a problem for Jesus to take the time to stop and heal the woman with an issue of blood, even though the situation with Jairus' daughter was critical. Jesus knew he could go back in time on behalf of Jairus' daughter—to before her illness. And that's exactly what Jesus did. Then he moved her into that present time. People will laugh at you when you talk about dominion over natural laws. Believe me, I know. When they see the miracles, they will stop laughing and you will become famous.

A major key to walking in miracles is to understand and take dominion over time. Look at the miracles of Jesus as presented in the gospels. Look at the words that are used to describe the timing of most miracles. They are immediately, straightway, that very hour, the selfsame hour and from that hour. This helps our understanding of the following Scriptures:

"And I will restore to you the years that the locust hath eaten, the cankerworm, and the caterpiller, and the palmerworm, my great army which I sent among you. And ye shall eat in plenty, and be satisfied, and praise the name of the LORD your God, that hath dealt wondrously with you: and my people shall never be ashamed" (Joel 2:25–26).

"The Spirit of the Lord is upon me, because he hath anointed me to preach the gospel to the poor; he hath sent me to heal the brokenhearted, to preach deliverance to the captives, and recovering of sight to the blind, to set at liberty them that are bruised, To preach the acceptable year of the Lord" (Luke 4:18–19).

Jesus said that he was anointed to preach the acceptable year of the Lord. The acceptable year of the Lord is the year of jubilee for his people. That is the year of restoration and the recovery of spoil on the missed increase because of what was lost. In *chronos*, or linear time, the year of jubilee would come only every fifty years. Because Jesus restored us to inhabit eternity by faith, then by faith every year is the acceptable year or the year of jubilee and restoration. We don't have to wait fifty years. We don't even have to wait fifty minutes! Jesus was anointed to preach that, and so are you and I.

We can walk in this revelation today as we produce fruit and live the God kind of faith. As we do, we will bring the good things of heaven down to the earth. Remember that if dominion over natural laws were not for us today, then Jesus would not have told Peter to come as he invited him to walk on water. Jesus did not say we should wait for a later time. Jesus restored us back to our original position of inhabiting eternity. If we choose to take dominion over time, we can have jubilee or restoration all the days of our life. Jesus will not choose for us; he leaves it up to you and me to decide for ourselves. I pray that you choose to walk in your full inheritance.

CHAPTER 4

DOMINION OVER TIME AND SPACE IN THE OLD TESTAMENT

Knowing about things to come, interpreting the times, and understanding divine appointments or seasons (*kairos* time) were available to the Old Testament saints by faith. Remember the woman of Canaan who took dominion over time and space, even though she was not under the old covenant?

The children of Issachar routinely operated in this anointing because they had a revelation that God is not limited by time. They knew he operated in and out of time and was always available in the now to give them wisdom by the Holy Spirit.

"And of the children of Issachar, which were men that had understanding of the times, to know what Israel ought to do; the heads of them were two hundred; and all their brethren were at their commandment" (1 Chron. 12:32).

We have access today to the timeless wisdom of God. We can receive by the Spirit of God wisdom for the future, wisdom from the past, and wisdom of the now as Jesus is the beginning and the end and is the I Am.

"He layeth up sound wisdom for the righteous" (Prov. 2:7a).

"But the Comforter, which is the Holy Ghost, whom the Father will send in my name, he shall teach you all things, and bring all things to your remembrance, whatsoever I have said unto you" (John 14:26).

"Howbeit when he, the Spirit of truth, is come, he will guide you into all truth: for he shall not speak of himself; but whatsoever he shall hear, that shall he speak: and he will shew you things to come" (John 16:13).

As we discussed in the introduction, God made Abraham the father of many nations, then went back in time and told Abram that his name was now Abraham as God had already (past tense) made him the father of many nations. When God lets us see things to come, we see them because they already exist. They are not seen in the present, yet they already exist in the future. To have them manifest in the natural, we call the things that are not in the present as though they already exist, because they do. Then we see them become real in this natural, three-dimensional world.

"(As it is written, I have made thee a father of many nations,) before him whom he believed, even God, who quickeneth the dead, and calleth those things which be not as though they were" (Rom. 4:17).

Perhaps no one is more famous for dominion over time than is Joshua. As the people of Israel battled the Amorites, they needed more daylight for a complete victory.

"Then spake Joshua to the LORD in the day when the LORD delivered up the Amorites before the children of Israel, and he said in the sight of Israel, Sun, stand thou still upon Gibeon; and thou, Moon, in the valley of Ajalon. And the sun stood still, and the moon stayed, until the people had avenged themselves upon their enemies. Is not this written in the book of Jasher? So the sun stood still in the midst of heaven, and hasted not to go down about a whole day" (Josh. 10:12–13).

Time stopped for almost a whole day. We need to understand how awesome our God is. God kept the whole universe running smoothly, even though certain orbits had ceased. If inhabiting eternity can stop time for a day, don't you think you can take dominion over time for your miracle money to arrive before it's too late?

Not only could people under the old covenant stop time, but King Hezzkiah made time go backward and had fifteen years added to his life. Think about this. We have a new and better covenant. Praise the Lord!

"In those days was Hezekiah sick unto death. And the prophet Isaiah the son of Amoz came to him, and said unto him, Thus saith the LORD, Set thine house in order; for thou shalt die, and not live. Then he turned his face to the wall, and prayed unto the LORD, saying, I beseech thee, O LORD, remember now how I have walked before thee in truth and with a perfect heart, and have done that which is good in thy sight. And Hezekiah wept sore. And it came to pass, afore Isaiah was gone out into the middle court, that the word of the LORD came to him, saying, Turn again, and tell Hezekiah the captain of my people, Thus saith the LORD, the God of David thy father, I have heard thy prayer, I have seen thy tears: behold, I will heal thee: on the third day thou shalt go up unto the house of the LORD. And I will add unto thy days fifteen years; and I will deliver thee and this city out of the hand of the king of Assyria; and I will defend this city for mine own sake, and for my servant David's sake. And Isaiah said, Take a lump of figs. And they took and laid it on the boil, and he recovered. And Hezekiah said unto Isaiah, What shall be the sign that the LORD will heal me, and that I shall go up into the house of the LORD the third day? And Isaiah said, This sign shalt thou have of the LORD, that the LORD will do the thing that he hath spoken: shall the shadow go forth ten degrees, or go back ten degrees? And Hezekiah answered, It is a light thing for the shadow to go down ten degrees: nay, but let the shadow return backward ten degrees. And Isaiah the prophet cried unto the LORD: and he brought the shadow ten degrees backward, by which it had gone down in the dial of Ahaz" (2 Kings 20:1–11).

God is not bound by time and, by faith, neither are we. God has always wanted us to inhabit eternity with him. He set it up that way from the beginning. Do you know how long Adam lived before his fall from the eternal realm because of sin? You don't know and neither do I. Why? The Scriptures don't tell us, because Adam inhabited eternity and did not live according to linear time. He was made in the image and likeness of God.

Once Adam sinned, he fell from a place of dominion over the earth to a place where time was his master rather than his servant. As a result, the Scriptures now tell us about seasons of time in our lives and how long people lived.

"To every thing there is a season, and a time to every purpose under the heaven: A time to be born, and a time to die; a time to plant, and a time to pluck up that which is planted A time to kill, and a time to heal; a time to break down, and a time to build up; A time to weep, and a time to laugh; a time to mourn, and a time to dance; A time to cast away stones, and a time to gather stones together; a time to embrace, and a time to refrain from embracing; A time to get, and a time to lose; a time to keep, and a time to cast away; A time to rend, and a time to sew; a time to keep silence, and a time to speak; A time to love, and a time to hate; a time of war, and a time of peace" (Eccl. 3:1–8).

"And the days of Adam after he had begotten Seth were eight hundred years: and he begat sons and daughters: And all the days that Adam lived were nine hundred and thirty years: and he died. And Seth lived an hundred and five years, and begat Enos" (Gen. 5:4–6).

Living under the bondage of time is part of the curse that came on mankind. Jesus redeemed us from the curse, so now we can inhabit eternity and have dominion over time.

CHAPTER 5

DOMINION OVER TIME IN NATURE

When Jesus took authority over nature, he did so by taking dominion over time. Let's look at some examples in Scripture.

"And the same day, when the even was come, he saith unto them, Let us pass over unto the other side. And when they had sent away the multitude, they took him even as he was in the ship. And there were also with him other little ships. And there arose a great storm of wind, and the waves beat into the ship, so that it was now full. And he was in the hinder part of the ship, asleep on a pillow: and they awake him, and say unto him, Master, carest thou not that we perish? And he arose, and rebuked the wind, and said unto the sea, Peace, be still. And the wind ceased, and there was a great calm. And he said unto them, Why are ye so fearful? how is it that ye have no faith? And they feared exceedingly, and said one to another, What manner of man is this, that even the wind and the sea obey him?" (Mark 4:35–41).

Notice that there was a great storm of wind and then there was a great calm. In natural circumstances, when a great storm begins to wane, it takes several hours for there to be a great calm. Normally the storm tapers off until, after a great while, things are calmer, and it continues to diminish in strength until finally there is a great calm.

Jesus took dominion over time and passed right over the time needed to produce a great calm. The storm went from the beginning to the end because Jesus is the Alpha and Omega, the beginning and the end. Based on Jesus' comments to the disciples, it is clear that we have the ability to take dominion over time and calm storms. He wanted to know why they had no faith. Dominion over natural laws is done by faith, as we believe that we too inhabit eternity like Jesus. As children of God, aren't we joint heirs with Jesus?

If we can rebuke natural storms, we also can rebuke the storms of life. We speak peace in the name of Jesus and the devil has to let go. Please understand that the storms of life come from the enemy. If Jesus brings the storms, then he won't rebuke storms. He rebukes storms because he is not the author of the storms.

Jesus won't bring a storm and rebuke it just as he won't make someone sick then heal him. He won't lead us into temptation then deliver us from evil. God is not double minded. Jesus will not divide his kingdom. In Mathew chapter 12, Jesus was accused of dividing his kingdom. As usual, Jesus had the answer of good news.

"Then was brought unto him one possessed with a devil, blind, and dumb: and he healed him, insomuch that the blind and dumb both spake and saw. And all the people were amazed, and said, Is not this the son of David? But when the Pharisees heard it, they said, This fellow doth not cast out devils, but by Beelzebub the prince of the devils. And Jesus knew their thoughts, and said unto them, Every kingdom divided against itself is brought to desolation; and every city or house divided against itself shall not stand: And if Satan cast out Satan, he is divided against himself; how shall then his kingdom stand? And if I by Beelzebub cast out devils, by whom do your children cast them out? therefore they shall be your judges. But if I cast out devils by the Spirit of God, then the kingdom of God is come unto you" (Matt. 12:22–28).

If Jesus had made one person sick and then healed, his house would have fallen. Jesus won't divide his kingdom by bringing sickness or storms or temptations into our lives. Satan won't divide his kingdom by healing, calming a storm or bringing deliverance into our lives. It's very simple. The devil brings the storms and Jesus, or his joint heirs, rebuke them.

When Jesus cursed the fig tree, he took dominion over time to speed up the decaying process.

"And on the morrow, when they were come from Bethany, he was hungry: And seeing a fig tree afar off having leaves, he came, if haply he might find any thing thereon: and when he came to it, he found nothing but leaves; for the time of figs was not yet. And Jesus answered and said unto it, No man eat fruit of thee hereafter for ever. And his disciples heard it. And in the morning, as they passed by, they saw the fig tree dried up from the roots. And Peter calling to remembrance saith unto him, Master, behold, the fig tree which thou cursedst is withered away" (Mark 11:14–14, 20–21).

Even if you cut the roots off a tree it would not wither and be dried up overnight. Jesus, through the words of his mouth, caused time to accelerate in that fig tree. We should show the world that the one who overrode time lives inside of us now, and we can override time. In the kingdom of God, there is no time.

Have you ever thought about what happens when someone is miraculously healed of cancer? The work of white blood cells and other healing properties God has put in our bodies are accelerated and the attacking cancer cells are slowed down or stopped until they are overwhelmed and totally defeated. This is accomplished through dominion over time in the eternal realm of the kingdom of

God. The blood of Jesus has restored us to a place of dominion over natural laws.

The first recorded miracle of Jesus was a good example of dominion over time in nature. The faith of Mary, the mother of Jesus, overrode time.

"And the third day there was a marriage in Cana of Galilee; and the mother of Jesus was there: And both Jesus was called, and his disciples, to the marriage. And when they wanted wine, the mother of Jesus saith unto him, They have no wine. Jesus saith unto her, Woman, what have I to do with thee? mine hour is not yet come. His mother saith unto the servants, Whatsoever he saith unto you, do it. And there were set there six waterpots of stone, after the manner of the purifying of the Jews, containing two or three firkins apiece. Jesus saith unto them, Fill the waterpots with water. And they filled them up to the brim. And he saith unto them, Draw out now, and bear unto the governor of the feast. And they bare it. When the ruler of the feast had tasted the water that was made wine, and knew not whence it was: (but the servants which drew the water knew;) the governor of the feast called the bridegroom, And saith unto him, Every man at the beginning doth set forth good wine; and when men have well drunk, then that which is worse: but thou hast kept the good wine until now. This beginning of miracles did Jesus in Cana of Galilee, and manifested forth his glory; and his disciples believed on him" (John 1:1–11).

When I was in Lyon, France, I toured a historic winery and learned about the making of wine. It takes several years until there is a finished product ready to drink. The very first step in the process is water, which prepares the soil and allows the vines to grow and produce grapes. Then after years of growing time comes the harvest time. After picking the grapes, you crush the grapes and press it into what is commonly referred to as "must." The must ferments until the sugar is turned to alcohol. Once fermentation is complete, clarification begins. Then the wine must be aged, some for a short time, others as long as two years. Finally, the wine is put into containers, distributed, and is ready to drink.

What happened above in the first chapter of John is that the winemaking process went from the beginning, the water, to the end, drinkable wine, as the time for growing and processing was eliminated because Jesus is the Alpha and the Omega. The process went from the beginning to the end without time. As your revelation of this truth increases, you will see that dominion over time is involved in virtually all miracles.

CHAPTER 6

TRANSLATIONS THROUGH TIME AND SPACE

"And when even was now come, his disciples went down unto the sea, And entered into a ship, and went over the sea toward Capernaum. And it was now dark, and Jesus was not come to them. And the sea arose by reason of a great wind that blew. So when they had rowed about five and twenty or thirty furlongs, they see Jesus walking on the sea, and drawing nigh unto the ship: and they were afraid. But he saith unto them, It is I; be not afraid. Then they willingly received him into the ship: and immediately the ship was at the land whither they went" (John 6:16–21).

Our natural mind has a hard time accepting the truth that dominion over time and space is available for children of God today. We say to ourselves that, after all, that was Jesus and he is God. But the Scriptures say that we can do today what Jesus did when he walked the earth.

"Verily, verily, I say unto you, He that believeth on me, the works that I do shall he do also; and greater works than these shall he do; because I go unto my Father" (John 14:12).

Let's look at the account where Philip performed the act of water baptism for the eunuch.

"And he commanded the chariot to stand still: and they went down both into the water, both Philip and the eunuch; and he baptized him. And when they were come up out of the water, the Spirit of the Lord caught away Philip, that the eunuch saw him no more:

and he went on his way rejoicing. But Philip was found at Azotus: and passing through he preached in all the cities, till he came to Caesarea" (Acts 8:38–40).

Philip was placed in the right place for the advancement of the kingdom of God and for the fulfillment of his kingdom destiny. Your faith may not be at the level to believe for physical translation to another physical place. Then start where right where you are. Can you believe God can and will bring about circumstances that place you on the right path and assignment in the natural in order to fulfill your kingdom destiny? The only difference between the two is that in Philip's case, it was done without time. Philip has no better spiritual DNA than you do if you are born again.

Sometimes God will translate people in the spirit and we can see things that exist in another place or time without him moving us physically. I have heard accounts in the life of John G. Lake where he saw details of things in Africa before he was ever physically there. The same thing happened to me. I give details about this experience in chapter seven of this book. God showed Enoch the end times, even during the days of the book of Genesis or the book of beginnings.

"And Enoch walked with God: and he was not; for God took him" (Gen. 5:24).

Enoch already saw the future as explained to us in Jude verses 14–15.

"And Enoch also, the seventh from Adam, prophesied of these, saying, Behold, the Lord cometh with ten thousands of his saints, To execute judgment upon all, and to convince all that are ungodly

56

among them of all their ungodly deeds which they have ungodly committed, and of all their hard speeches which ungodly sinners have spoken against him" (Jude v.14–15).

Enoch saw the glorious return of our Lord Jesus Christ thousands of years before it will happen. He had no New Testament from which to read about it. Enoch could see it because it already exists. He merely saw what already exists further along in linear time. It doesn't exist in his time or in our time as yet, but it is real nonetheless. It just hasn't manifested into this three-dimensional world as of this time. That's why when God gives you a word of wisdom, you can know that what he said will come to pass because it already exists. As far as God is concerned, it has already happened.

Sometimes God just gives instructions about things to come, as he knows the future because he inhabits eternity. Cornelius and Peter experienced this in Acts chapter 10.

"There was a certain man in Caesarea called Cornelius, a centurion of the band called the Italian band, a devout man, and one that feared God with all his house, which gave much alms to the people, and prayed to God alway. He saw in a vision evidently about the ninth hour of the day an angel of God coming in to him, and saying unto him, Cornelius. And when he looked on him, he was afraid, and said, What is it, Lord? And he said unto him, Thy prayers and thine alms are come up for a memorial before God. And now send men to Joppa, and call for one Simon, whose surname is Peter: He lodgeth with one Simon a tanner, whose house is by the sea side: he shall tell thee what thou oughtest to do" (Acts 10:1–6).

"While Peter thought on the vision, the Spirit said unto him, Behold, three men seek thee. Arise therefore, and get thee down, and go with them, doubting nothing: for I have sent them" (Acts 10:19–20).

Taking dominion over time and space is not just for certain people whom God has selected. Just as healing and salvation are for whosoever will, inhabiting eternity is for whosoever will. Elijah was raptured or translated to heaven. The Bible says that he was just like you and me. Not only was he translated, he also took dominion over nature.

"Elias was a man subject to like passions as we are, and he prayed earnestly that it might not rain: and it rained not on the earth by the space of three years and six months. And he prayed again, and the heaven gave rain, and the earth brought forth her fruit" (James 5:17).

"And it came to pass, as they still went on, and talked, that, behold, there appeared a chariot of fire, and horses of fire, and parted them both asunder; and Elijah went up by a whirlwind into heaven" (2 Kings 2:11).

The various "raptures" that people refer to that are in the Bible are really translations through time and space into heaven. Seven such raptures or translations to heaven are found in the Word of God:

1. Enoch

2. Elijah

3. Jesus

4. The Church

5. The Great Multitude

6. The 144,000

7. The Two Witnesses

CHAPTER 7

PERSONAL TESTIMONY

Remember that I told you I had seen ahead in time what was going to happen after my arrival in Kenya, Africa? In a vision, I saw myself standing in the middle of what appeared to be an empty building. Suddenly, over one hundred children surrounded me. They pressed in to get close to me. I bent down on one knee and began to lay my hands on them, speaking blessings and deliverance over them. At the time that I received this vision, I had never been to Kenya, nor did I know that what I had seen was in Kenya.

Several years later, when I was in Kenya, I recognized the empty building I had seen in the spirit. I had been in that building on previous trips, but it always had room dividers for classrooms or it was full of people for a church service, so I didn't relate it to the empty building in my vision. On this day, however, I recalled the vision from God. It was late in the day and I was walking through the building alone. As I reached the mid-way point, or thereabouts, a great many children were coming toward me, reaching out to me to touch me. Because I had already seen what I was to do, I did not shy away or just walk through the children while saying "God bless you." There was the same number of children as I had seen in the vision. I kneeled down to touch each one and spoke a blessing over each one, breaking every curse over their lives, including the curse of poverty. I knew that what I had done would make a big difference in their lives, and I still believe it to this day.

I don't know how much time passed as I prayed for each child. I do know that in the natural, it had to have been a very long time as I was completely worn out by the time I had finished. Because God's people in Kenya are such servants—there was always someone around me to serve me, always seeking to tend to my needs, even to the point of carrying my Bible for me everywhere I walked. Except when I retired for the evening, they never left me alone for more than a few moments. Yet, during this ministry over the children, I was unaccompanied and unassisted. I knew that as I obeyed God to bless the children, time has been slowed down to accomplish the will of God.

Sometimes we must take dominion over time to bring blessing and deliverance to people. Other times we may need to do it to keep us out of trouble because we have messed up. That is what happened to my wife Sandy and me in Lyon, France. I was there on a business trip and was blessed to be able to bring my wife along with me. It was time to return home, and we had train tickets to take us to Paris, where we would board a plane back to Houston, Texas.

We checked out of our hotel in what appeared to be plenty of time. The hotel called a cab for us and it soon arrived to drive us to the train station. We had a difficult time explaining where we wanted to go to the taxi driver. We couldn't speak French and he couldn't speak English. Finally, I remembered the word for train in French and said, "*la gare.*" We rode along just as happy as we could be, totally unaware that there are two train stations in Lyon. The driver dropped us off and we walked to the ticket counter to check in. The woman who was there to help us spoke English, and I was feeling really good as I could see that we had time to spare.

Things turned sour as she examined our tickets and explained to us that our train departed from the other train station. She explained that it would be impossible to make it to the other station in time to catch our train. She informed us that a taxi ride would take about forty-five minutes. I asked her if there was another train leaving from the station where we were or a later train at the other station that could get us to Paris on time to make our flight. Our hearts sank as she gave us the bad news after examining all the schedules through her computer.

Sandy and I sat down and looked at each other, and then she said to me, "Honey, what are we going to do?" I straightened up and told her that we were going to use our faith. I had been studying about taking dominion over time and space and all the things of this natural world. We quickly prayed and called the things that were not as though they were. We declared that we had dominion over time and we would be at the right train station and even have to wait on the train.

We jumped up and quickly hailed a taxi. I knew if we wanted God to do what we can't, then we had to do what we can. We do the possible; then he does the impossible. We do the natural then believe him for the supernatural. As the driver helped us load our luggage into the trunk, I asked him how long it would take to get to the other station. He said about forty minutes. I thought to myself, that's five fewer minutes, and now all we need is to have a forty-minute drive become a twenty-minute drive. We just might make that train if we are fortunate enough to find our departure gate right away when we arrive.

As we drove through the city of Lyon, I began to feel a little bit of anxiety. I knew the anxiety was not of God, so I meditated on Isaiah 57:15 and inhabiting eternity. I put all my cares in God's hands and declared that I had taken dominion over time and that we will be waiting on that train. As we continued, everything seemed normal, just like any other car ride. The traveling speed was normal and we just watched the streets, the buildings, and the countryside as we rolled along. I didn't look at my watch, and both of us sat in silence until the taxi slowed to a halt. We had arrived at the right station. I looked at my watch and, glory to God, it had only taken fourteen minutes!

We gathered our luggage, paid our fare, and walked into the terminal. The first thing we saw was a big sign indicating the location of our gate. It was nearby and we scurried to get there, found a seat up front, and there we were, waiting on our train. We had to wait for exactly five minutes. Later, when we boarded our plane in Paris to fly home, we reflected on what God had done and how good it felt to be on our way back to the good ol' United States of America. Hallelujah!

Remember that through faith in the name of Jesus we too can unscramble eggs, because by faith we can inhabit eternity, even while we are still on this earth.

The revelation that we have dominion over time helped me to be a better father. It took me from the position of having failed my daughter to that of a faithful father.

In 2005 my daughter Debbie took the National Board Dental Hygiene examination which, when passed, would enable her to practice as a licensed dental hygienist in the state of Texas. Debbie had asked me to pray for her while she was taking the test. She wanted me to pray that the Holy Ghost would bring to her memory all the things that she had studied. She relied on her father to watch over her and pray for her.

After the test, she told me that she didn't feel so good about how well she did on the exam. To my horror, it hit me that I had not prayed for her during the test. I felt so remorseful. How could I have forgotten?

I turned to the Lord to help me be a godly father for my daughter. He reminded me that I have dominion over time. By faith, I took dominion over time, prayed for my daughter, and declared it retroactive to the time of the examination. I received the revelation that at the linear time of the test, God, who inhabits eternity, already knew that I would pray a retroactive prayer. He responded during the test just as if I had prayed at that linear time. God is moved by faith. You and I can inhabit eternity on the earth and we can unscramble eggs just as God can! It takes faith, and Jesus calls it great faith.

For your information, she scored a 97.5 on the test, which was one of the highest scores in the state. Praise the Lord! She worked hard and studied hard and she is the one who deserves all the credit. I'm just making the point that I went back in time so that my prayers were not too late.

You may find my last personal testimony recorded in this book the strangest of them all. Again, if God did not want us to walk in dominion over natural laws he wouldn't have said "come" to Peter inviting him to walk on water. Rather than saying, "come" he would have instructed Peter to wait until he gets to heaven. Jesus didn't instruct Peter to wait until he is in heaven for dominion over natural laws, and he is not instructing us that way either. Jesus is the same yesterday, today and forever and no respecter of persons so we have the same invitation as Peter received. Jesus is saying to us to come and take dominion over natural laws. We don't have to wait until we get to heaven! God wants us to take dominion over natural laws while we are still on the earth.

I was hurt by someone whom I love. I had a hard time dealing with the hurt because of the sadness that it brought. I took dominion over time and by faith moved my heart back in time before the time that I received the hurt. Then, by faith, my heart moved forward into the present, but now without the hurt. My mind didn't forget what happened, but the pain was gone and I never struggled with forgiveness for that person again.

What is the difference between what I just described and Lazarus' body going back in time to before his illness? Then his body came forward in time with no pain and no decay. My heart came forward with no pain and no decay. You can do the same. This revelation can help you put physical bodies back together, relationships back together, and marriages back together. Anything the devil has broken you can put back together by faith through dominion over time.

CHAPTER 8

IT'S NOT TOO LATE FOR YOUR DESTINY

What you say about you means more than what everyone else says. All you have to do is agree with God. What do you say? The devil and the world say that you are going to fail, and God says you are going to succeed. Whichever one your tongue agrees with is what determines what will come to pass. Agree with what God says about you.

Even people with great authority don't always say the right things about you. In fact, people of great authority on a particular subject often say stupid things, even in their area of expertise. Below are some examples of quotes from people of authority.

"Everything that can be invented has been invented." (U. S. Patent Office Commissioner Charles Duell, 1899)

"The horse is here to stay, but the automobile is only a novelty–a fad." (The president of the Michigan Savings Bank advising Henry Ford's lawyer Horace Rackham not to invest in the Ford Motor Company, 1903)

"The telephone has too many shortcomings to be seriously considered as a means of communication." (A corporate memo from Western Union, 1876)

"The wireless music box has no imaginable commercial value. Who would pay for a message sent to nobody in particular?"

(Response from associates of RCA founder David Sarnoff, circa 1920s, when he proposed investing in the young radio industry)

"Television won't be able to hold on to any market it captures after the first six months. People will soon get tired of staring at a plywood box every night." (Twentieth Century Fox studio boss Darryl F. Zanuck, 1946)

"There is no reason anyone would want a computer in their home." (Ken Olsen, President of Digital Equipment Corp., 1977)

"Get rid of the pointed ears guy." (NBC television executive to Star Trek creator Gene Roddenberry, 1966, recommending the new show eliminate the Vulcan character Mr. Spock)

"That kid can't play baseball." (Milwaukee Braves minor league manager Tommy Holmes, 1952, appraising Henry Aaron, who went on to hit 755 home runs in the major leagues)

"You aint going nowhere, son. You ought to go back to driving a truck." (Grande Ole Opry manager Jim Denny, 1954, firing Elvis Presley after one performance)

"You will never amount to very much." (A Munich teacher to a ten-year-old Albert Einstein, 1889)

The only real authority on anything is Jesus. He says that you are more than a conqueror. He says that you are not going under because you are going over. He is the only real authority. He is the Word and the Truth.

"And it came to pass, when Jesus had ended these sayings, the people were astonished at his doctrine: For he taught them as one having authority, and not as the scribes" (Matt. 7:28–29).

Remember our discussion about Enoch? He was a man of flesh, yet he saw the end of time all the way back in the time of the book of Genesis. He could see it because it already exists. In the spirit realm, we too can see the past and present of linear time. Linear time is a creation of God and placed in the earth by God along with all the other natural laws.

"And God said, Let there be lights in the firmament of the heaven to divide the day from the night; and let them be for signs, and for seasons, and for days, and years"(Gen. 1: 14).

Spiritual or supernatural laws override natural laws. Surely, we can believe supernatural laws to override natural laws when we know and understand that a natural law can override another natural law. For example, the law of aero-dynamics overrides the law of gravity. The law of aerodynamics says that the law of gravity can be counteracted if you combine the right shape with the right speed and the right weight. That is why the law of gravity will not cause airplanes to fall to the ground as long as adherence to the law of aerodynamics is observed.

God has already seen your destiny because it already exists. If Enoch could see the end of the age, certainly God Almighty can see to the end of your life. God has already planned and seen your destiny, and he does not make any mistakes.

"For I know the thoughts that I think toward you, saith the LORD, thoughts of peace, and not of evil, to give you an expected end" (Jer. 29:11).

God has already provided everything that you will ever need to fulfill your kingdom destiny. The entire reservoir of heaven has been placed inside of you, and it is accessed by faith. The kingdom of God is in you and it is manifested into this three-dimensional world from the inside out. That means that no outside circumstances can stop you, because your provision doesn't come from the outside. It comes from the inside. If you want more, all you have to do is speak more.

God inhabits eternity. He knows what your needs are today and he knows what your needs will be tomorrow. Before I prayed for my daughter about her test, God knew what I would be praying and believing for, even from the foundation of earth, because he inhabits eternity.

"And it shall come to pass, that before they call, I will answer; and while they are yet speaking, I will hear" (Isa. 65:24).

Below is a true story (verified on truthorfiction.com) as told by Helen Roseveare, a medical missionary from England to Zaire, Africa. This extract is taken from *Living Faith* by Helen Roseveare (ISBN 978-1-84550-295-9) Christian Focus Publications, Fearn, Ross-shire, Scotland, http://www.christianfocus.com.

"One night, in Central Africa, I had worked hard to help a mother in the labor ward; but in spite of all that we could do, she died leaving us with a tiny, premature baby and a crying, two-year-old daughter.

We would have difficulty keeping the baby alive. We had no incubator. We had no electricity to run an incubator, and no special feeding facilities. Although we lived on the equator, nights were often chilly with treacherous drafts.

A student-midwife went for the box we had for such babies and for the cotton wool that the baby would be wrapped in. Another went to stoke up the fire and fill a hot water bottle. She came back shortly, in distress, to tell me that in filling the bottle, it had burst. Rubber perishes easily in tropical climates. "...and it is our last hot water bottle!" she exclaimed. As in the West, it is no good crying over spilled milk; so, in Central Africa it might be considered no good crying over a burst water bottle. They do not grow on trees, and there are no drugstores down forest pathways. All right," I said, "Put the baby as near the fire as you safely can; sleep between the baby and the door to keep it free from drafts. Your job is to keep the baby warm."

The following noon, as I did most days, I went to have prayers with many of the orphanage children who chose to gather with me. I gave the youngsters various suggestions of things to pray about and told them about the tiny baby. I explained our problem about keeping the baby warm enough, mentioning the hot water bottle. The baby could so easily die if it got chilled. I also told them about the two-year-old sister, crying because her mother had died. During the prayer time, one ten-year-old girl, Ruth, prayed with the usual blunt consciousness of our African children. "Please, God," she prayed, "send us a water bottle. It'll be no good tomorrow, God, the baby'll be dead; so, please send it this afternoon." While I gasped inwardly at the audacity of the prayer, she added by way of corollary, " ...And while You are about it, would You please send a dolly for the little girl so she'll know You really love her?" As often with children's prayers, I was put on the spot. Could I honestly say, "Amen?" I just did not believe that God could do this. Oh, yes, I know that He can do everything: The Bible says so, but there are limits, aren't there? The only way God could answer this particular prayer would be by sending a parcel from the homeland. I had been in Africa for almost four years at that time, and I had never, ever received a parcel from home. Anyway, if anyone did send a parcel, who would put in a hot water bottle? I lived on the equator!

Halfway through the afternoon, while I was teaching in the nurses' training school, a message was sent that there was a car at my front door. By the time that I reached home, the car had gone, but there, on the veranda, was a large twenty-two pound parcel! I felt tears pricking my eyes. I could not open the parcel alone; so, I sent for the orphanage children. Together we pulled off the string, carefully undoing each knot. We folded the paper, taking care not to tear it unduly. Excitement was mounting. Some thirty or forty pairs of eyes were focused on the large cardboard box. From the top, I lifted out brightly colored, knitted jerseys. Eyes sparkled as I gave them out. Then, there were the knitted bandages for the leprosy patients, and the children began to look a little bored. Next, came a box of mixed raisins and sultanas - - that would make a nice batch of buns for the weekend. As I put my hand in again, I felt the...could it really be? I grasped it, and pulled it out. Yes, "A brand-new rubber, hot water bottle!" I cried. I had not asked God to send it; I had not truly believed that He could. Ruth was in the front row of the children. She rushed forward, crying out, "If God has sent the bottle, He must have sent the dolly, too!" Rummaging down to the bottom of the box, she pulled out the small, beautifully dressed dolly. Her eyes shone: She had never doubted! Looking up at me, she asked, "Can I go over with you, Mummy, and give this dolly to that little girl, so she'll know that Jesus really loves her?"

That parcel had been on the way for five whole months, packed up by my former Sunday School class, whose leader had heard and obeyed God's prompting to send a hot water bottle, even to the equator. One of the girls had put in a dolly for an African child -- five months earlier in answer to the believing prayer of a ten-year-old to bring it "That afternoon!" "And it shall come to pass, that before they call, I will answer; and while they are yet speaking, I will hear" (Isaiah 65:24).

God already knows what all your future needs are. He has made provision for them and they are waiting on you to call them into existence into this three-dimensional world. They are inside of you and come from the inside out.

"Neither shall they say, Lo here! or, lo there! for, behold, the kingdom of God is within you" (Luke 17:21).

Don't be afraid that you don't have what it takes to fulfill the dreams that God has placed inside of you. You have a purpose given to you by God, and he has equipped you to do everything that you are destined to accomplished. He has put everything you need inside of you! Don't think that you have run out of time or it is too late. Remember our discussion of Amos 9:13 in chapter 2? Go back and reread the end of the chapter if you need to. You can accomplish in a short time what used to take much longer in these last days, especially as we take dominion over time.

"Behold, the days come, saith the LORD, that the plowman shall overtake the reaper, and the treader of grapes him that soweth seed; and the mountains shall drop sweet wine, and all the hills shall melt" (Amos 9:13).

You may have been too afraid to dream. You may have buried your dreams because of hopelessness. I declare in the name of Jesus that it is time to dream again. What is it that keeps trying to come up in your heart, even though you try to ignore it? It is time to really live again, for without a dream or vision the people perish.

We all have a dream or vision, even if it's buried so deep in our heart that it has become as dead. It is something that God plans for us to do and to be. I call it forth to live through resurrection power in the name of Jesus. By faith, I send your heart back in time when the dream was alive and call it forth into the present. Joseph's father, Jacob, who later became Israel, asked Joseph an important question. He said in Genesis 37:10, "What is this dream that thou hast dreamed?" I ask you the same question right now. What is this dream that you have dreamed? I believe the Holy Ghost will bring it to your memory or create it brand new in your heart. The time is now to walk in your destiny.

God has not placed a dream in your heart to frustrate you, but to fulfill you. We walk by faith according to the promises of God, yet we have to put our hands to something. God cannot bless the work or our hands unless our hands are working. God does all the hard part, but God works with us. We start right where we are with what we already have. If all you know is the first tiny step, then just be faithful right where you are and take that first step.

"For a dream cometh through the multitude of business; and a fool's voice is known by multitude of words" (Eccl. 5:3).

You will find that you will enjoy working with God, even when you are confronted with problems, because God does all the hard part. We just have to be faithful and trust a good God who has already told us the outcome. There is no need for anxiety when you already know of a wonderful outcome, even if you don't know how you are going to get there.

I am a University of Texas graduate. I love to follow the Texas Longhorns, especially in football. In the 2006 Rose Bowl for the national championship, the Longhorns were faced with fourth down on the USC five-yard line with under a minute to play, and they were trailing by five points. The game hinged on the next play. The national championship was riding on this one play. My stomach was in knots as they approached the line of scrimmage because I didn't know the outcome. What if they failed? Much to my delight, Vince Young glided across the goal line for the game winning touchdown.

I have watched a replay of that game many times. Everything is the same when I watch the replay except for one item. Now I know the outcome. The excitement is still there, but there is no anxiety because I know the Longhorns will get the victory in the end. I really enjoy watching the whole game, even when I see negative plays that set them back, because I know the final outcome is victory. That is why God wants you to know your final destiny, not just after you die, but your victorious destiny on this earth. When setbacks come, we just keep going forward, working on our dream

74

that we already know is a reality. We know the victory is ours and we are not too late!

When we dream we can enjoy our lives, even when we have to face adversity. We rely on God to do the hard part. We just keep moving as we look at what we are going to instead of what we are going through. We don't worry because we know the outcome. This enables us to think about others instead of always thinking of ourselves. We don't have to lose our integrity, because all we have to do is please God, not man. God is a lot easier to please than man is. People see our joy and it glorifies God.

"When the LORD turned again the captivity of Zion, we were like them that dream. Then was our mouth filled with laughter, and our tongue with singing: then said they among the heathen, The LORD hath done great things for them" (Ps. 126:1–2).

Remember, God has already given you everything you need to fulfill your kingdom destiny. The whole kingdom of God is available to you to access by faith. Because we have dominion over time and space, we can enter heaven and bring to earth all the good things of the kingdom of God. They are manifested in the natural from the inside out. Since our provision comes from the inside out, outside circumstances do not effect our provision. Outward circumstances cannot stop us, because our provision comes from the kingdom of God that is within us. It doesn't matter if the economy is weak or strong. A bad economy cannot stop your provision, because our economy is external. It doesn't matter how the economy is doing, or who is in office, or what the price of oil is, or how high the tax rates get, or how much healthcare might cost, or if the stock market is up or down. None of these things can change the fact that everything you will ever need has already been given to you, and it all will come from the inside out.

"According as his divine power hath given unto us all things that pertain unto life and godliness" (2 Pet. 1:3a).

Taking dominion over time and space as when Philip was translated, taking dominion over gravity as when Peter walked on water, or receiving a word of wisdom like Joseph is no more supernatural than physical healing or sowing and reaping with finances.

Remember that you have dominion over all the natural laws placed into the earth because you inhabit eternity, because you have no end. If you are born again, you will live forever with Jesus, and the devil can never take that away from you. Walk in your kingdom destiny. Put into practice the revelation that you have dominion over time and space and let Jesus say that you have great faith. As you walk in the corresponding miracles, you will bring blessing, healing, and life to others, and God will be glorified through your faith.

How wonderful it will be to hear the greatest words that any man, woman, boy or girl could ever hear from Jesus.

"His lord said unto him, Well done, thou good and faithful servant: thou hast been faithful over a few things, I will make thee ruler over many things: enter thou into the joy of thy lord" (Matt. 25:21).

"Remember the former things of old: for I am God, and there is none else; I am God, and there is none like me, Declaring the end from the beginning, and from ancient times the things that are not yet done, saying, My counsel shall stand, and I will do all my pleasure:" (Isa. 46:9-10).

What others are saying ......

I approached it with somewhat of a cynical attitude. However after reading this I found it to be very inspiring and in every way Biblically correct. This is a great work and I will recommend it to others.

Mort Petrushansky, Associate Pastor
Shalom Hebraic Christian Congregation

"Pastor David Hope's book Inhabiting Eternity On Earth brings reality to the concept of a time machine. Using biblically sound principles, Pastor Hope points out that faith in the Lord Jesus Christ brings the believer into the realm of eternity - a realm that is not bound by the dimensions of time and space. This book brings out the truth that when we place ourselves in Christ by faith, we place ourselves in the One who not only travels through time but is the creator of time and is the master of it."

Tom Battle
Sr. Pastor, Lord's Glory Church

"This book Inhabiting Eternity On Earth by David Hope will stir your faith to greater heights and possibilities. His own personal stories together with the story of the hot water bottle and the doll are never to be forgotten. It is soundly scriptural and supported with solid illustrations from the word of God. I read it in one sitting. I highly recommend it to you as a challenge to your faith. You will grow in knowledge and develop more spiritual understanding than ever before. Don't be destroyed for a lack of knowledge."

Gerald Davis, D.D.
Overflowing Cup Ministries

Other books from David Hope

The Goodness of God

God's Perspective on Money

Do you want to be Healed?

Other Books from RevMedia Publishing

Almost Out of Grace by David Yanez

Military Life and the Power of God by David Yanez

How to Function in this Economy by Gerald Davis

To order more books of INHABITING ETERNITY ON EARTH or any other of the books on this page. Please visit our website www.revmediapublishing.com

You can also visit your local bookstore or online book merchant

Prayer for Salvation

Life is not as complicated as most people think. If you are in covenant with Jesus, all you have to do is please him and everything else takes care of itself. Trust in God and make him your source of supply and by faith you can live on earth like it is in heaven.

"Therefore take no thought, saying, What shall we eat? Or, Wherewithal shall we be clothed? (for after all these things do the Gentiles seek) for your heavenly Father knowth that ye have need of all these things. But seek ye first the Kingdom of God and his righteousness; and all these things shall be added unto you."(Mt 6:31-33)

Those that have entered into a blood covenant with God by being born again by the spirit of God have eternal life and can walk in health and prosper.

"Beloved, I wish above all things that thou mayest proper and be in health, even as thy soul prospereth."(3Jn2)

Remember, God does not automatically heal and prosper you. We have to call upon his promises in the name of Jesus. Every good thing comes to us through Jesus. The only qualification to receive from the Father is that we know his Jesus. We have to have made Jesus our Lord and Savior.

Every one needs Jesus because our sins have separated us from a holy God. There is not anyone who has not told a lie or committed a sin. God, however, is holy and cannot fellowship with sin.

So he sent his son, Jesus, to be a man and pay for our sins that we might have the righteousness of God.

Jesus took on our sins and by faith we can receive the exchange of his righteousness and therefore boldly enter into the throne of grace. It's not based on what we have done but what Jesus has done for us. If you will receive Jesus, you will never have to be ashamed again, for Jesus will not be ashamed of you.

"For both he that sanctifieth and they who are sanctified are all of one: for which cause he is not ashamed to call them brethren."(He 2:11)

Because of the sin of Adam, we stand condemned until we receive Jesus by faith. Jesus did not come into the world to condemn the world but to set us free from the condemnation we are already in. It is a free gift of God. We simply receive it by faith.

"Therefore as by the offence of the judgement came upon all men to condemnation: even so by the righteousness of one free gift upon all men unto justification of life. For as by one man's disobedience many were made sinners, so by the obedience of one shall many be made righteous. More over the law entered, that the offence might abound. But where sin abounded, grace did much more abound: That as sin hath reigned unto death, even so might grace reign through righteousness unto eternal life by Jesus Christ our Lord."(Ro 5:18-21)

If you have never received Jesus into your heart but you would like to, then pray this prayer and mean it in your heart. You will inherit eternal life and can begin walking in your inheritance by receiving provision and health on this earth in the name of Jesus.

Lord Jesus, I am a sinner. Forgive me of my sins, come into my heart and make me brand new. Wash me clean in your precious blood. I confess you as my Lord and Savior and I will serve you all the days of my life. Jesus, thank you for saving me and I thank you that I am now a child of God and my name is written in Heaven. I thank you that I now can call upon your name for healing and provision. Help me to make you my source of supply for every area of my life.   AMEN

Prayer for Healing

Jesus wants you healed. All we have to do is ask and believe his word.

"And Jesus departed from thence, and came nigh unto the Sea of Galilee; and went up into a mountain, and sat down there. And great multitudes came unto him, having with them those that were lame, blind, dumb, and many others, and cast them down at Jesus' feet; and he healed them: insomuch that the multitude wondered, when they saw the dumb to speak, the maimed to be whole, the lame to walk, and the blind to see: and they glorified the God of Israel."(Mt 15:29-31)

You see, it's the healing that glorifies God, sickness only glorifies the devil. You can still glorify God when you are sick but God is never glorified in sickness. Great multitudes came to Jesus and he healed them all. To me a multitude of people is as many people as the eye can see. A great multitude of people is more than that. Great multitudes are even more than that. Yet Jesus did not turn even one person away but healed them all.

Some people think that God won't heal them because of some bad things they have done. Healing is for whosoever will receive it by faith. It is not based on performance. Don't you think that in great multitudes that there is at least one person whose performance is worse than yours? Yet, Jesus healed them.

In great multitudes you will find every kind of person. You'll find rich and poor, young and old, and every ethnic background. In great multitudes, there are educated people and those with no schooling, people from good families and people from bad families. There are those that are married, singled and divorced. There are people with religious training and people who have never even prayed before. There are kind people and mean people. There are people who are sexually pure and those that have performed perversion. There are all kinds of people. Jesus healed them all.

God desires greatly for us to receive our healing. Jesus took 39 stripes on his back so that we could be healed. Jesus will never say no to your healing. If Jesus wanted to say no, he wouldn't have had to take one stripe. He didn't take stripes on his back to say no, he took the stripes so that he could say, YES! Pray this prayer out loud and believe God for healing.

Father,

I come to you in the name of Jesus. I give you thanks that by your stripes I was healed and I receive it now by faith. I speak God life and resurrection power into my body to make me whole from the top of my head to the soles of my feet for the glory of God. I release my faith for it and count it as already done in the name of Jesus. Amen.

Please visit us at Metro Church....

David Hope is the Senior Pastor of Metro Church, a non-denominational, spirit filled, family church located in Humble, Texas. If you're in the Houston/Humble area please join us for service.

Metro Church
7811 FM 1960
Humble TX 77346

Service Times:
Sunday Morning 10:40am
Sunday Evening 6:00pm
Wednesday Evening 7:00pm

www.emetrochurch.com

Notes

Notes

Notes

Notes

www.ingramcontent.com/pod-product-compliance
Lightning Source LLC
Chambersburg PA
CBHW062017040426
42447CB00010B/2027